Advance Praise for

I SING : THE BODY
Poems about Body Image

"These poets grapple with self-image and self-doubt as they lay bare their identities. Their poems capture the struggle between what we are told and what we believe about ourselves, what is imagined and what is real. They are alive with memory and anger and hope. I dare you to read these powerful poems and not feel the feelings of your own childhood pain or teen angst once again. But it will also remind you that you are not alone and that you have the power to mend yourself—and hopefully, as Jenn Givhan concludes, 'You would see who you are / & marvel.'"

—Sylvia Vardell, author of the ALA bestseller
Poetry Aloud Here and co-editor of *The Poetry Friday Anthology*
and *Poetry Friday Power Book* series

"I SING : THE BODY is a miracle of diverse voices speaking truth and life into the too often unheard songs of the body and heart."

—Chris Baron, author of *All of Me*,
a middle grade novel-in-verse about body image,
and professor of English at San Diego City College

There is no one body. There is no one poem. In I SING : THE BODY, the many bodies resonate in the many poems. Like our bodies when we arrive in them, these poems are all "Beautiful beams from the inside out." Sometimes we may not be ready to see the light; sometimes the lights sees us, all of us. I say stand up as you read this book, move your body as the poems move through you. You will never end up in the same place. You will only be beginning.

—Crag Hill's next book, co-edited with Todd Fuller,
is *Level Land: Poems For and About I35*
(forthcoming from Lamar University Press)

I SING : THE BODY
Poems about Body Image

Juventud Press

an anthology edited by René Saldaña, Jr.

Juventud Press

Juventud Press
Copyright © 2021 by René Saldaña, Jr.
ISBN: 978-1-953447-77-7
Library of Congress Control Number: 2021940745

Published by Juventud Press
an imprint of FlowerSong Press
in the United States of America.
www.flowersongpress.com

Cover Art by Melina Melgoza
Cover Design by Priscilla Celina Suarez
Set in Adobe Garamond Pro

I SING : THE BODY
Poems about Body Image

an anthology edited by René Saldaña, Jr.

in memoriam
Irene C. Herrera
June 12, 1943 to January 30, 2021

TABLE OF CONTENTS

PREFACE

LILIANA VIDAURRE (LV): It hasn't always been like this, though, being happy with myself, that is. Poised. In charge of myself. Back in the day, huh? I wish I could put into words where I was in my life—emotionally, physically, and spiritually—with my body positivity journey before pageantry found me. Words are hard to come by because those were some hard times back then, but our stories, I think, are important to tell. Instead of talking about just the pain, I want to tell about how I found myself in Plus Size modeling and eventually pageantry.

There was a lot of character shaming when I was younger. My confidence took a hit on a daily basis. I remember being in middle school and laughing at this boy's jokes because I thought he was so funny. Maybe it was also a kid crush. I'm not sure, but I did think he was funny. And maybe I was paying him a bit of extra attention. His friends got wind that I was doing this and teased him so bad: "Hey man, we hear the fat girl likes you." I saw it in his face right away, the embarrassment, He couldn't look at me. I felt embarrassed for him. And I just wanted to disappear. I stayed away from that boy after that. But there did come a day when people trying to tell me I should be embarrassed about how I looked just weren't hurtful anymore. This change didn't happen overnight, though. It was a long road.

I regained my self-respect with pageantry, and I also gained a new tribe of like-hearted women, my new tribe who understood my journey. We all have different stories about our journeys getting here today, but the struggle's the same.

JENNIFER O'NEAL JACKSON (JJ): Pageantry's helped me to see how intentional and individual our journeys are. Pageantry has been a sanctuary for me. Not an inner source of religious habit likened to one who chases crowns. Pageantry presented me with an opportunity to become emboldened, to intentionally strip away layers of insult that had accumulated over decades, to rid myself of this image imposed on me by others, to overcome all that negativity the daily bombardment can, at times, bring on. Pageantry strengthened my inner core which began to radiate externally while I moved across pageant stages.

Then the crowns came that gave me a platform that attracted other women and men who were broken who needed someone to look at, to look to, to look with. Yes, people needed to see others like themselves who have overcome.

That is the power of a testimony. I'm a person of faith, so when the Bible, which is the foundation I stand on, tells me to love others as I do myself, I take it to heart. I'm not just throwing scripture here; instead, I work to live it in my daily walk as a ministry to show that God created us all beautiful. But people can also be ugly-mean and no matter that God made us all His children, some folks are just plain mean and will let you know what they think of you, to your face or behind your back. But, ultimately, God will not let you be put to shame. I am His willing instrument. This message is for the young and the young at heart. We all can overcome personal and social stigmas. My weight and size as a 6'0' tall, 3-something weighing woman, that is my outer self, will never be the gist of who I am. I am also my own inner perceptions. The Lord has shifted my perceptions. I can say now, after years of feeling ashamed and imprisoned by that shame, I am free. So can we all.

SANOE TUITELE (ST): I remember back in middle school wearing basketball shorts, baggy clothes just to cover my big body. Did I think I was beautiful? No. Did I think I was cute? Yes. What's the difference? Beautiful beams from the inside out. And that's exactly what I didn't have, which almost brings tears to my eyes. I felt cute because I was in fashion. I was trendy to all the girls around me. So they didn't bother me so much. Just so long as I was wearing the right clothes. I didn't like what I was wearing, but during that time, the trend of baggy clothes was considered cute by the in-crowd. I compared myself quite often to my friends who looked nothing like me. They were all much skinnier, they all had boyfriends, and here I was this big Polynesian girl trying to blend in, and the way I did that, to some extent, was to hide my body behind baggy clothes. But by hiding, it was easier for them to not see me.

So, Dr. J., you're talking about actual crowns. The ones we've earned in pageantry over the years. But crowns work on a different level, too. I call them tokens of beauty. Gems or little pieces of brightness that people bestow on someone else, and these tokens are transformative. Looking back at this moment in my life when I experienced a transition of feeling cute to being beautiful. It didn't dawn on me then that I was beautiful, inside and out. I didn't start thinking of myself like that till I was about 23 years old, and some people are like, "Oh, but you're so beautiful. Why did it take you that long for you to realize it?" But transformation doesn't happen from one day to the next. Not after decades of getting it from every direction every day about how I didn't fit in. It's like the whole time I just thought I was cute. But beautiful? Nah. I just thought I was enough to fit in with everybody else, even if it meant just barely fitting in, like on the outskirts of the crowd, you know?

Along that road, though, I did see and even meet people I knew beamed beautiful from the inside out. They wore those tokens of beauty like a crown. It was people like a teacher I'm thinking about. I don't mean this person was like drop dead gorgeous; it meant that this person had a heart, had this compassion for people, and it was like, she radiated beauty because she cared and wasn't scared to show it. You know, she actually was concerned about my safety. She actually made me feel safe. So that kind of person beams beautiful. For me, that teacher made me feel like it was okay for me to be unique, I was okay to be different. It was like a realization. I love that trait beaming from within me. That's one example of the little tokens of beauty that I picked up along the way, and when I finally built the courage to say that I was beautiful in the mirror, it was because I took along all those little pieces from these beautiful people I've met in my life from small kid time to my adulthood. And that's what I truly believed: that I was beautiful, that nobody could tell me nothing else, that if somebody even told me I was ugly, well, I wasn't. I was brightness, I beamed. I was—am beautiful.

Today, here's how I think: if this is what being beautiful means, well, I'm going to take every little piece that I can and share it all along the way. It's like the tables have turned...people look to me for inspiration. It's a humbling experience, but it wasn't easy. None of it has been.

LV (TO SANOE): You were such a pretty little girl. I look at pictures of you as a girl, and you were adorable. I wish I could travel back in time and hold you tight to remind you it was ok to feel nervous. No matter what the others said or did didn't mean that there was anything wrong with you.

It's silly, but I've been in the plus size industry for over 10 years now, and I'm brave enough to be honest. We've got to be if our hope is to make a difference, to share those tokens of beauty with others. I love that—tokens of beauty.

One time I was going to be in a fashion show representing their plus size and they chose two dresses for me they wanted me to walk out in. One of them did not zip up. I asked her if she could switch that dress for another dress, and she told me to stop eating for a few days to fit into it. "And if that doesn't work?" I asked. She said, "Then you'll only wear one dress for the show." I made the dress fit. Kind of sad, isn't it, that we're made to feel like if we don't fit then we don't fit.

JJ: I was loving listening to Sanoe. I was like, tell me more. I think my slant comes from a different perspective. I came from a family where, you know, many of the other women presented like there wasn't ever a problem. You know, we didn't say we loved you a lot, but you just knew that you were loved. Not a one of them ever told me I was beautiful. They just thought I should know I was.

I came up where we were churched (if I can say that to you), and a lot of people, when you go to church, you read about how God loves you, and people should love you, and you should love other people, but then when you get out of church and you go to school, you see everything different. Unfortunately, a lot of the things that we were told in church were God's way, they're not exactly what I saw in school or any other place.

My transformative moment is clear in my memory. To let others see God's love through me and through my actions. I decided one day that I wanted to live in that love, be that love, be that every day for others. I learned that sometimes people don't always do right, and a lot of times those of us on the receiving end, we wear the insults, and they weigh heavy on a body. Kids can be very mean, and I learned that very early in life, from a distance really. Honestly, I didn't have a lot of people who bullied me a lot in that way, but when I talked to people, I didn't know who I was. I didn't know what my beauty was. I didn't know what that meant and how that would impact my life going on from the child I once was.

Just to segue a little bit. I went on to work over the past few years as I sit on the board of an anti-human sex trafficking organization, and now more than ever, I know the significance of reaching back to young girls, ages 10 to 14, or even between 8 to 12. Now we could get to them and tell them that predators prey on people who don't see how beautiful they are, because the first thing they do is they start appealing to them where they are, and then they draw them out. And then *there's somebody...there's this older person who really likes me, he likes me for me*, and all these things, and I learned. When I reflect back to when I was a child, how much I really didn't know who I was, I really didn't know those things myself, and it was stuff that I was told, but I just at that age I didn't understand what should've been plain. The one thing I need to get across here is that young people are getting it—you're beautiful—and understanding what we're saying to you. Our duty to young people as moms, aunts, grand-mothers, pageant winners is take time to teach that, to make sure through being that love that they have an understanding because situations are coming now that are forcing children to have applied understanding when they get in situations that are coming directly at them.

And so, my angle, from my experience, growing into myself is learning that my beauty wasn't like others'.

LV: You talked about this idea of growing into yourself, and I'm imagining you're talking about emotionally growing?

JJ: Mostly, yes. A lot of that growth is spurred by the physical, though. I was 5'10" at a young age, and all the younger girls my age were dating all the taller guys, and none of the taller guys wanted a lanky country girl who, you know, who looked like I was coming from here and lanky. It took me a while because I didn't fit in. But God, you know, as I got older, I learned what my fit was. I keep thinking, if I'd had someone back then telling me plainly to take my time to learn who I was and to understand that my mistake was thinking I didn't fit but based on someone else's definition of fitting.

But if you take charge of the definition-making, you're always going to fit. You're not meant to fit others' standards; your beauty is individual, and it has to be, you know, you have to have people there, and that's what I kind of wanted to submit to this story, that we four are here for you to stand on our shoulders and see what we see in you. It's understood, you're not gonna look like everybody else. I was a late bloomer. I was a late, late bloomer. I didn't find out about my beauty until around 24. But I came to the same slow realization as Sanoe's: "Hey, Jennifer, you know, you've always had that scar right there, you've always had this, and that makes you distinctive! Your hips make you, they remind you of your grandmother!"

It's okay to slow things down and realize I don't have to be socially and physically like everybody. I was made to be uniquely me, myself, and I. And for me to get to that place of understanding, it took a lot of village for me, and that's what I want to provide for the young people who read this book, who read the poetry, to know that there are people who are willing to be a part of a healthy village to help them see they are made beautifully...

uniquely, originally themselves.

ST: I like that, Dr. J: a lot of village. And not always who you think should be part of that village. I still remember the day I cried in the bathroom at Summer Fun camp because someone called me fat! I remember looking in the mirror and constantly telling myself, "I'm going to be skinny. I just have to be." Later, the Summer Fun Park Director hit me with his words so hard they stung like a slap across the face: "Your boobs are supposed to be bigger than your stomach!" He was supposed to be part of my village, but he wasn't in the least.

JJ: You just made me fill up with all of this love and memory because my grandmother passed away about 10 years ago, and you just fill me up with so much joy, because right now you are my reflection. I woke up one morning, we were staying with my grandmother, and I walked into the kitchen where she was baking fresh biscuits (she liked to make everything from scratch), and I watched her—like her, I wear my hair up in buns—she had her hair pulled up in a bun on the center of her head, and she had her apron around her wide hips, and she was this tall, beautiful woman; and as she stood there in her environment inviting me in, I felt welcomed. Like, I'm a part of this. I felt so much joy to see this woman I looked like, and she was so graceful, and what she did—because she knew exactly, intentionally, everything she did—and it gave me so much hope. Because my grandmother, when she turned 60, did not know how to read, and she had us write her letters, and for every letter that we wrote for her, she would send us a quarter or a dollar. But she fit. Unlike that director, my grandmother was my whole village.

I remember that day when I finally came into the kitchen after seeing her write me! My grandmother got her GED. You have to understand, she used to sign her name with an "X," and I remember when I came for a visit, and I got that same sense of being filled with joy that I felt earlier listening to these stories. She knew how to read. She was in her kitchen, and I was there at the doorway, and there was no conversation that took place. I kind of eased into the kitchen, and she kind of nodded me on over where she was rolling out the dough, and she was making this amazing food, and it's the most amazing, surreal experience...I'm ready to cry, and I'm telling you as a grown woman, I remember reflecting as a child on how beautiful that was that I knew that if she could do what she did, I could do whatever I wanted to do, and everything I've done since has been devoted to her because I knew I could make it when everything looked impossible because she taught me to be confident in who I am, she taught me to define myself. My village is made up of a strong lineage of women who did a lot and sacrificed a lot! And she did that for us because we ended up leaving home to come stay with her. And she raised me.

She did that for me. She was amazing.

When she passed, all of the church people came to her house to eat. All the people, even though it was her job to clean their houses! That was her work. But they saw her for who she was in life. A sister. Through her actions, she taught me, "Don't worry about all that, take care of your family, be confident in who you are, and know that you're made beautifully."

And in those quiet, no words exchanged moments that I remember, I don't remember her talking directly to me because I was young. I just remember watching her and feeling like she's beautiful. And she had the hips, she was tall. And she was amazing. And she was talented. And that's the well where I draw from. It wasn't about degrees for me and never has been. All the degrees I could get in the world never meant anything, as long as I knew I was reaching my capacity and doing the best that I could do, that I, one day, would make her into a legend because that's what she was to me.

LV: Adina, you're present. You've been really quiet, and I'm wondering if you've got those same sorts of beauty token stories or any sort of experience that you'd like to share with us.

ADINA POLLARD-SIMON (APS): All of us have similar stories, but for me, I came from what we will consider a ghetto, a high-risk community. I like to keep it real. In my community when I was born, I was a chubby baby. But as I grew, my weight fluctuated. It was up and down. But I have these three persons I like to always say were very instrumental in my life. These three women taught me how to be strong. And none of it had to do with my weight.

My mother, my Godmother, and also my grandmother, who I spent most of my years with. But like with other high-risk communities, in addition to these strong women, I also had neighbors and friends who looked out for me. But raising me it was mainly my poor mother, and later it was my grandmother and her taking turns.

Even though I'm an open person, there are some parts of me I keep in here, right? But I know I'm supposed to share those parts because I like to motivate and inspire people through my stories. But it's not all the time you want to open up. Right? But I have some parts of me I like to keep hidden; I know, though, if it is to help somebody through this book, I don't have a problem. However, though my grandmother was not a plus size person I still have great admiration for her. She was a very short woman, and she was not from this country, Trinidad. She was from Grenada. She came to Trinidad at a young age, and there's a lot of attributes that I would say I took from her. Among them, how to do battle against odds.

My grandmother couldn't read for the life of her. She never had an education, but she taught us how to pray. She was a really faithful woman. Knew her Bible backwards and forwards. And she guarded that word in her heart. Let me tell you, for somebody who couldn't read, if you were reading the Bible in front of her and you mispronounced one word in the Bible, she would stop you right there and correct you. That amazed me about that woman! I always said to her, "Granny, you sure you didn't go to school? Every word you read from Genesis to Revelation is right."

As time passed, when I became a first-time mother, and like happens often, of course my weight fluctuated, up and down. After a few years, going to church helped me realize we in my coumtry really don't have a problem with plus size. Men really adore us. That is a fact. I have had some bad experiences. For example, a few taxi drivers I've hired have told me, "You're too big, you'll have to pay for the seats next to you." Like taxis are "One size fits all!" but I'm not that ideal size they're thinking of. But on the whole, I feel very at home in my body. It fits me, and I fit it.

One size does not fit all! That annoys me. Right? And our experiences in pageantry prove that.

ST: I decided to join pageantry in the March of 2018. I felt worthy enough to put myself out there for all plus size women. I felt I could be the change I wanted to see in the world. I knew that I was unique because I was irreplaceable. In this whole wide world there is no one else like me. My uniqueness proves out my beauty. My resilience in life has helped me to be strong but compassionate. I've learned to be bold but humble. To love me before loving others, in order to love others. Finding your true beauty starts from looking within. Finding what makes you beYOUtiful.

LV: I have also found myself reflecting a great deal on this journey. My pageant mother, Mama Nanette, pulled me out of a very dark place when I was brought into the pageant spotlight. I had been told by extended family members that they were glad my grandmother and father were not alive to see what I had become. I was told that they felt sorry for my husband for having to deal with me, and another person told me that the spirit of Jezebel lived in me.

I was broken and tired of being judged. All I wanted to do was quit it all and hide, but then I was found and pulled into MPW by an angel who saw more in me. The first year all I could to do was cry and wonder what made me so worthy to be standing among such impressive and dignified women. I was inspired and motivated. And when I returned after my first pageant week I gave the world all I had because I felt like that was the least I could do after being given a crown to wear. Let me tell you, I was so excited about my first crown that I wore it in the Georgia airport on my way home! Bad idea —the airplane didn't have enough height to the ceiling. I remember wearing it to certain events in my community and having to really fight the fears of being judged. I mean, wearing the crown in public was a statement of ownership: This is me. Deal with it.

I went back to pageant week the second year and I found joy in reuniting with the family who gave me meaning. I felt more worthy now. I had done some more work in the Plus Size industry and felt like I had earned the right to be there.

When I was selected the second year to be part of the MPW court I experienced another level of joy in myself. Something like self-assurance. By then, I was certain that I was wanted and loved, and this was and continues to be. Daily I discover a whole new love for myself. I am not afraid what others think they see in me. I'm not embarrassed anymore. I don't get sick like I used to when people chose to judge me. I know now that those who judge me do not understand what it is that my soul is searching for.

I went to get measurements for a photo shoot I'm doing next Monday, and I was told that I've grown two inches around my hips and bust, but that I'd stayed the same around my waist. Some would be devastated with this news. In my younger days, I would've been. But I thought I must be doing something right. In the past ten years of my modeling journey I have learned that staying healthy doesn't necessarily mean smaller...skinner; it just means doing the right things for my body. I love buying good, fresh foods, and I love staying active doing things that keep me happy. I've added physical activities to my hobbies. Here's my secret: Do right by yourself. Healthy is happy, and happy is healthy.

JJ: I believe there are internal scars that we who have dealt with the shaming have that remind you of where you once were.

LV: And recognizing the shame leads us to teaching our society how a woman no matter her shape or size should be looked up to, despite the scars. Or maybe to spite the scars.

Finding the confidence to shine has been a long and sometimes difficult journey. Not everyone understands why it's so important to feel noticed. See me, I feel like screaming. The whole of me. Aqui estoy y no me voy. I share my platform with like-minded and like-hearted women now who have allowed me to feel not only not shy, but excited to showcase my beauty. Because God made us all beautiful, and we all look different and yet we share a lot of the same struggles. I've got to say, it feels like we're digging, we're digging, and we're digging here.

APS: True. Like we're only scratching the surface. But as former Ms. Plus World queens we do have certain responsibilities.

Like I've said, I don't like to talk about the negative! Isn't there already so much of that in the world around us? Why add to it? Well, maybe we need to sometimes share even what makes us uncomfortable to be, like Sanoe said earlier, the very change we want to see in the world. All this digging has been very fruitful.

I'll finish by saying, to me, every person is important and unique. We might not all look the same way, much less the way others think we should look. Some of us not the size the magazines say is the right size. All those fashion magazine covers saying it's the skinny bumpers who are the ideal. What color skin, or style of hair is right. And if we fall for that trap, well, we get all this ugly judging by others. Or, we can say it is who we are, one different from everyone else, that makes us beautiful. My mantra is "See positivity." In everyone. Everyone means every single one of us. That means doing. It's action. It's an individual purposefully doing the action: seeing all the positive, seeing all the beauty. And when we think we won't find it, like Liliana says, dig again and again and again. I like to call it a challenge. Of course, we in life, we go through a lot of stuff; but I like to be known as someone who is always looking for positivity.

See positivity. Do positivity.

THE COURT OF QUEENS

DR. JENNIFER JACKSON is a true product of the Piney Woods of East Texas. Affectionately known as Dr. J., at a young age Dr. Jackson knew she wanted to help keep the world well. After attending Longview High School, she graduated from Prairie View A&M University with a degree in Biology & Chemistry. Holding true to the childhood vision she embraced, Dr. Jackson went on to attend Hampton University School of Pharmacy where she earned her Doctorate in Pharmacy in 2008. She currently lives and practices in Tyler, TX. Her impact is global. She serves her immediate community as a Pharmacy Manager/Pharmacist for Wal-Mart, a Texas College Adjunct Professor, and as a member of many service and social organizations. She is the Founder/CEO of Triumvirate.

Dr. Jackson was crowned Ms. Texas American Elegance Woman 2015-16 and went on to win the National Crown/Title Ms. American Elegance Woman 2016. In November 2016, she was titled International American Elegance Woman 2016-17, Mrs. All World Beauties 2018, Ms. US Plus Intercontinental 2019, and went on to win the Ms. Plus Intercontinental 2019 title to inspire women globally to Be the Glo.

Dr. Jackson is the proud wife of Apostle Laramie Jackson I and the mother of Laramie "LJ" Jackson II and Yasmine. Together they shepherd the Temple of Deliverance and Healing International Worship Center where she serves as Senior Pastor.

ADINA POLLARD-SIMON is Miss Plus World Trinidad and Tobago National Director, pageant producer, and founder. She resides in the beautiful, twin island Republic of Trinidad and Tobago where she is known to many as "Queenie." Multitalented, well-rounded, outgoing, loving, and extremely ambitious, Adina began making appearances and performing on stage at the age of thirteen in school choir. Raised by her grandmother, she entered competitions consistently making yearly contributions that helped her to adapt and advance to different stages throughout her music career. Adina believes in encouraging persons to assert themselves by motivating, inspiring, and educating women to aspire for higher reaches. As a mother, career woman, and grandmother she always makes time for church, her family, and still finds time for community and cultural work.

Adina has been creating history over her 16 years in Plus Size Pageantry, having graced fashion runways, worked with many local designers and pageant directors, participated in charity events, hosted and judged pageants and talent shows. She was selected to represent Trinidad and Tobago at the 12th Annual World Championships of Performing Arts in Hollywood, CA, in 2008 where she performed against competitors from over 40 countries in singing, modelling, and a variety of other arts. In addition to competing in national pageants in her country, in the Caribbean, and other international pageants, she holds prestigious titles of Miss Plus Size Trinidad and Ms. Plus Intercontinental Humanitarian Ambassador—Trinidad and Tobago in 2019-2020.

Passionate about personal development, Adina understands the strength of pageantry and its accompanying sisterhood. She advocates for networking that can create growth resulting in empowerment.

SANOE TUITELE was born and raised in the state of Hawai'i, specifically on the island of O'ahu. The daughter of Elizabeth and the late Tony Tuitele, she identifies as Hawaiian, Samoan, Caucasian, Chinese, and Puerto Rican Spanish. Sanoe graduated from Radford High School in 2011, and in December 2016 she graduated with a Bachelor in Science from Hawai'i Pacific University.

Currently, she is a Special Education Teacher at her alma mater.

In 2018 she joined the Miss Hawaii Plus Pageant and was crowned Miss Hawaii Plus 2019 and advanced to compete in the Miss Plus World Pageant. She returned home with the title of Miss Plus World 2019-2020. Her goal is to continue to empower the youth locally and globally to follow their dreams.

LILIANA RAMIREZ VIDAURRE was born and raised in the Resaca City of San Benito, TX. She began her modeling career a decade ago. Since, she has been featured in magazine spreads, fashion shows, and on runways. She has worked with a number of well-respected names in the fashion community, including Bec's Fashions, World Plus, Rent a Dress, Isabella & Jacque, and Aboveandbeyond Designs. Her work has also included art modeling for local colleges and art leagues. She has worked tirelessly in these places to shine a positive light on body image to help women in her community as a positive and inspiring voice. In addition to modeling she enjoys doing community service when possible and safe to do so; she loves to garden, cook, and travel. Liliana helps with the daily business of running FlowerSong Press with her husband, Edward. She is the mother of a beautiful fifteen-year old daughter, Luisa Isabella, who loves carnivals, and is taking boxing lessons. Liliana joined the pageant world in 2018 where she served as Miss Rio Grande Plus World for 2019 and Miss Plus World Humanitarian Ambassador for 2019-2020.

INTRODUCTION

Years ago I got to listen to poet Gwendolyn Brooks perform her work. If I remember correctly, I was sitting on a gymnasium floor cross-legged. I was a graduate student, but that day I was a kid, if you get my meaning. I'd read through much of her work leading up to her visit to Clemson, where I was studying, and fell in love with her now-classic "We Real Cool." As you can imagine, I was awestruck when she performed it. After, she took questions. I wanted to know, "Ms. Brooks, are you a poet first, or are you Black first?" I was working out my own identity as a writer and as a Chicano academic. I was genuinely curious, though maybe a bit of a romantic and so likely I hoped she'd say, "I am a POET!" Instead, she looked right at me from her place at the lectern and said, "Honey, I was born Black." And that, as they say, was that.

*

This book was originally going to be called About Face. I meant it as a sort of play on the words. First, implied in the title was the 180-degree turn. I wanted to present poems to readers that showed how these artists had themselves made that shift in thought. Bullied for being too dark, too big, too skinny, too this, too that, they could've ended up defeated; instead, they took the ugliness of bigotry aimed at them and turned tables on both it and the hateful people hurling it. They would not let themselves be ridiculed, made to feel unworthy, inferior. I wanted young readers to be similarly empowered, to know that they were not on this long row to hoe alone, that there were fellow travelers who would buttress them through their words. To show that they, too, could turn on a dime in the opposite direction. The other reason I wanted to call it About Face was metaphorical: face standing in for the body as a whole. This book, these poems would be about the face, that is, the body.

For years I had dreamed of putting this anthology together. I'd been calling it this from the start, pitching it to editors under this title, but now, when I started collecting all these wonderful submissions and reading through them, losing myself in them, I realized that the title wasn't working for me anymore. Missing from this title was the greater reason for putting this book together in the first place: the celebration of the self.

*

During my undergraduate years, I studied Walt Whitman's poetry. In his different works I found the sort of rebellious tone I had longed for that I didn't get in school-sanctioned, required reading. He encouraged me to "re-examine all" that I'd ever been told. For Whitman, there didn't exist dichotomies. Everyone was beautiful, everyone was a miracle. My friends and I would go around campus quoting lines from his work, yelling them at one another: "Do I contradict myself? Very well then I contradict myself, (I am large—I contain multitudes)," "I celebrate myself, and sing myself," "One's-Self I sing, a simple separate person," and "I sound my barbaric yawp over the rooftops of the world." Reading the poems in this anthology I find a similar spirit of celebration of the self, and so it makes sense to call it after his work. As a matter of fact, I can't call it anything different now, anything but celebratory, in praise of one's-self.

*

In junior high I found on a shelf a collection of short prose called *Stories from El Barrio* by Piri Thomas. In it, I found a story called "The Konk" about fourteen-year-old Piri who "had grown tired of [his] curly hair being called 'nappy,' pasas (raisins), or pelo malo (bad hair)." One day, he goes to Roy's Barber Shop where a konk or hair-straightening treatment would cost him $5, "SATISFACTION GUARANTEED." Roy attempts to dissuade him, telling him "he's got lots of good hair to work with," threatening that a konk "can burn your scalp right down to the bone," and finally warning that "If you want white man's hair, there's a price you gotta pay." Here readers understand that Roy is not referring to the $5 price tag, but a greater price, costing a piece of one's soul. Young Piri goes ahead with the treatment never the less. And burn it does. But in the end, he's gotten rid of the curly, nappy hair. Treatment complete, he "ran [his] fingers through [his] hair. It was like fine silk." Looking in the mirror, he concludes, "I was sure looking fine."

That good feeling doesn't last long, though. When he gets home, "Papi shook his head. He knew what my hurting was all about." His mom hugs him close

2

and lets him cry his "tears of hurt and shame." The very next day, playing out on the street, he's realized his mistake and is "sporting the baldest head in town."

*

"Sticks and stones may break my bones, but words will never hurt me"— whatever fool came up with that old adage is a fool of fools. Or an idealist, someone who looked at life through rose-colored glasses. Because words, especially when repeated and over time, are sure to break a spirit. Hurled at a child? Worse. Hurled by a child at a child? Don't even. Because where'd that child learn to be so mean in the first place?

*

I'm a person of faith. I grew up reading the Bible. One of my favorite stories in it is the story of Creation, where God made man in Their image. Fashioned him out of mud. And, here's my favorite part, God "breathed into [Adam's] nostrils the breath of life," and in that moment, Adam "became a living soul." A higher order of creature than any other in the animal kingdom. Then God made Eve from one of Adam's rib-bones: in other words, out of his marrow, and in that marrow, God's breath of life and every DNA sequence there would ever exist since Creation. Which is to say, genetically we all can trace back to those earliest of days. Our DNA theirs, theirs ours. In our marrow, Eve, Adam, and God's very breath of life. This is important because in the Bible, in the Old and New Testaments both, we are admonished that God is love, we are commanded to love our neighbors as ourselves. We are reminded that there "is no other commandment greater than these." But why use words like *admonished, commanded, reminded*? These words, it seems, are words of rebuke. Of getting after someone. I use these words purposefully, though, because also in our souls there is the capacity to do wrong, another trait we inherit from the first mother and father. It's no hard work to choose to do the wrong thing. It's harder to choose to do right. But dig it: in our own marrow (yours and mine) there is the breath of God: God is love, so should we be. Love our neighbors because love trumps hate. Love ourselves because we are God's children, and God doesn't make mistakes. God made us beautiful. We are miracles unto ourselves. And don't let anyone tell you different: we've been beautiful dating back to day one of humanity. Why not let's give love then? Just give love.

*

This takes me back to Gwendolyn Brooks' response to whether she thought of herself as poet first, or Black first. She said, "Honey, I was born Black." She said so being a Black woman visiting the South. Said so openly. Proudly. Leaving no doubt in my mind: we are born who we are born. Everything else we choose to become. I choose pride and joy in myself. I choose pride and joy in your self.

So, from the rooftops sound with me our proud and joyful barbaric yawps that, coincidentally, sound very much like in the Spanish: ¡soy como soy, y que! (That's my nod to another great and fine poet, Raquel Valle-Senties from Laredo, TX). A loose translation: *I am how I am, so what you gonna do about it! That's what I thought: you aine gonna do jack because it's me in charge of me. Me, myself, and I. Period!*

That's what's what!

*

For this anthology, I've had the great honor of selecting work by a variety of poets. Among them you'll find work by poets very well-known in the Young Adult field: Joseph Bruchac, Margarita Engle, Nikki Grimes, Linda Sue Park, Carmen Tafolla, Padma Venkatraman, and Janet Wong. Every one a great poet. You'll also find works by many poets classified as literary; that is, folks publishing for an adult reading audience, starting in the lit mags and journals, and progressing to books of their own. These are too many to mention here. Rodney Gomez, Julia Perez, and Melina Melgoza contributed visual poems (and you'll find Melgoza's work gracing the cover, as well). Though I'd seen visual poems before, I'd never really read them until I was challenged to consider not just what these looked like but also what they were speaking. There are some first-time poets on the list, too. One I'd like to mention is Paloma Muniz-Ochoa, who was, unbeknownst to me, 11 years old at the time of submission and acceptance.

I'm honored that these poets answered the call for submissions because if anyone can speak to pressing issues of the day, it's poets. Thanks to them all.

*

I conclude this introduction with essential Whitman: "I exist as I am, that is enough." As it should be.

—René Saldaña, Jr.
August 2020

I SING : THE BODY

Poems about Body Image

Josephine Cásarez
BROWN TRENZAS ARE FOR MENSAS

Come, Tom, said mother.
Are you ready, Betty?
Run fast, Betty.
Go home to mother, Flip.

Mira, Amá, soy Betty.
Soy Betty.
See my blonde hair?

No eres Betty, sonsa.
Eres Pepa.
Ya quitate esa toalla de la cabeza.
Eres Pepa, no Betty.

Look, Mother.
Look at Flip.

Qué es Flip, mija?

Ma, Flip es el perro de Betty.

Tu perro se llama Chihua, mija, no Flip.

Chihua?
My dog's name is Chihua, not Flip?
I have a dog named Chihua.
Ma, why can't I be like Betty?
I want blonde hair like hers.
And,

I want a dog named Flip.
She is sooooo cool.

Andale,
ponte a estudiar tu tarea, Be-t-t-t-ty.
Cuando crezcas
puedes nombrar a tus hijos
Tom, Betty, y a tu perro le pones Flip.
Pero right now, eres Pepa, no Betty.

Betty, Ma, soy Betty.
Mira mis trenzas amarillas.
I want to wear a coat and hat like Betty, Ma.
Y quiero trenzas amarillas.
Why don't I have yellow hair?
¿Por qué no tengo pelo amarillo, Ma?
Yo quiero ser como Betty.

Ya me cansas con tu Betty.
Betty no es de deveras.
Ella nomás vive en tu libro.

Where's father?
¿Por qué el papá de Betty usa suit,
y Apá no?

Acuérdate cuando fuimos al entrierro
la semana pasada,
él usó un suit.

Al trabajo, Ma, al trabajo!

¿Por qué no tenemos una casa como ellos?
Mira, Ma, mira su casa.
¿Por qué la mamá de Betty no suda?
¿Por qué ella 'ta blanca y yo no, Ma?
¿Tomara mucha leche?

Si,
y tú tomas mucho chocolate.

Comensando mañana, Ma,
yo voy a tomar mucha leche.

Vas a tener que tomar mucha leche.

Yo no quiero trenzas cafés.
Yo quiero trenzas amarillas
porque brown trenzas are for mensas.

Enedina C. Vásquez
BAD HAIR

I used to sit between Abuelita's legs
On hot summer days
And shed a tear for every yank she gave my hair.
A las niñas siempre se les hacen trenzas,
Así apretaditas
Para que no parezcan pajuelas greñudas,
She would say in a raspy old voice
As she wove my hair into long braids
As tight and painful
As the sins I used to confess
At the church of the Apostles Peter and Paul.
And I
Swore that when I grew up
I would cut off all my hair
And suffer no more.
And,
When *Apá*
In a drunken stupor
Would take off his black leather belt
To punish me for any offense.
Like,
The time I broke a dozen eggs
Or,
When I threw up the hamburger I was eating
During one of his fights with *Amá*
Or,
Just because he was drunk,

Those times
He would make me stand in the doorway of the kitchen
And ask me to walk across the room
While he whipped his belt across my thighs.
It would hurt for a while
Then,
I would go into the bathroom
And cut my hair.

Like,
During *mea culpa* days
Growing up Catholic
Thinking that nuns were perfect
And bald,
I took pride in cutting my hair
Shorter than my brother's.
Until one day,
As I listened to Sister Cabrini
Tell me that good Catholics
Knew all of the correct answers
In the Baltimore Catechism Manual
And I noticed a strand of hair
Pop out of her starched white veil
Wet with sweat
And how it just hung over her brow
I knew then that some things were not right.
I went home,
I cut my hair.

In college,
During one of those heated war protests
Or,
When the students were killed in Mexico City's riots
And *Apá* said they got what they deserved,
Or,
When Kennedy was assassinated
On the Thursday I started my period
And I hated all the blood,
Went into my room,
I cut my hair.

And when I wanted to ring the bell
During Sunday Mass
Just like Tony could do,
Dressed in his red altar boy outfit
That I thought would look better on me
And I was told girls were not allowed to ring the bells
Or help with Communion
Or go near the altar,
I cut my hair.
My braids were pinching my temples,
Giving me headaches
I wanted to help Father Fitzgerald
Give out the body of Christ
Or hold the Baby Jesus for all to kiss.
I wasn't allowed
Because I was a girl,
Less worthy,
And I believed it.
It has taken me a lifetime
To learn I don't have to cut my hair,
That no one will braid my hair again,
That no one will hit me again
And,
That if I can't be part of something one hundred percent,
I will take my leave because it is not for me.

I will never cut or braid my hair again
I will let it blow in the wind
Color it any color I want
Let it flow down my back
Pin it up to one side
And flaunt it
Because it is mine and I have no bad hair days.

Margarita Engle
¡AZUCAR!

When I was little, all the princesas I drew
looked like Celia Cruz, not Barbie.

Big hair, warm-hued skin, and wide Cuban hips.
Now I've grown into my own natural form,
avocado-shaped.

One day, a boy I don't know approaches me,
grinning as he announces, you're okay
in the front, but you look like a pear
from the back.

The force of his judgment stuns me,
a lightning strike that numbs my sense
of self.

For at least a year, I walk around feeling
like someone else.

Then, slowly, I recover, remembering
that in Cuba, gordita was a compliment,
even though in California chubby
always means ugly.

Gradually, I learn how to send my mind
rising up into sweet air, where it can hover
between places, so that someday,
somewhere, maybe
I'll be able to belong

inside the power
of a song.

Offbeat.
Unusual.
Different.
That's
me.

Giana Gallardo Hesterberg
ANDANDO

In 6th grade, Frank
with the green eyes
took one look and asked,
¿Quieres andar conmigo?

I nervously said
Sí,
confused when he
took my hand, interlocking
my fingers with his

Later he took me
behind the portable,
tongue soft like innocent
experience,
then carried my books to class

Girls, learn now–
don't say *sí*
if you don't understand
the question.

Mason Nunemaker
PEACH

I dared to eat a peach
let the juice run down
the corner of my mouth
drip from my fingers
skin between my teeth

I took a bite from the middle,
the plump juicy center
it tasted wonderful
so sweet & so cold

I held the pit in my hand
examined it closely to find
the smallest bits I missed
sucked the flesh out from
between the grooves & cried

But not because I felt guilty
I did not feel guilty for eating this time
this time I cried because it was gone
& it was such a relief to feel good

Despy Boutris
BAPTISM

My mouth is full
of riverwater.

And my name always comes out
like an apology.

Years ago,
before my brother's baptism,

I pulled back
my hair and pretended

to be a boy—
chest flat, hips narrow

with girlhood. Then
my mother rouged my lips

and brushed out my hair,
let it curl around my neck

like a noose.
Now I christen myself

in the river. I duck underwater
and become water,

not woman. I become bodiless
and fail to drown.

Rodney Gomez

EXCAVATION

Carmen Tafolla
A THOUSAND YEARS

Mama says I'm too fat.
Tía says I'm too skinny.
My brother says my hair's too bushy.
I think my hair's too straight.

At school I feel that I'm too short
but when I'm near my cousin Lupe,
I feel like a tall, gawky giant.
Lupe's skin is like pale peaches
and the tips of her hair have gold streaks
while my skin's so dark the tough girls at school
call me *La Prieta*, and Sammy next door just laughs
and says he can't see me at midnight.

Grandma catches me staring at Lupe's skin
and she can tell what I'm thinking.
—*Why can't I have skin like pale peaches?*
I ask her later, when we're alone in the kitchen
and only the cake on the table can hear us.

—*Then who would have skin*
like creamy dark chocolate?
And who would want to live in
a world with no chocolate?

I'm still frowning, as she begins to frost the cake,
rainbow sprinkles over chocolate fudge.
—*The girls with dark chocolate faces are NEVER*

on magazine covers, or starring in movies, I pout.
—Well, they SHOULD be, she insists.

Why can't I just be tall and slim, and skin like pale peaches
and hair with gold tips? And teachers would smile at me
that special way when they think you're so cute and so smart
(just because of the way you look OUTSIDE your skin?)

Later that day, after the dishes have been cleared from the table
and the birthday cake all eaten down to just crumbs, a smidge of
chocolate fudge, and one sliver of white peach from the filling
that didn't make it onto the serving spoon,
I hear Lupe complaining to Grandma.
I hate my skin, she says.
Kids at school call me La Guera! *and* La Gringa!
*And I don't look anything like the Virgen de Guadalupe
for whom I was named. She's a beautiful cinnamon chocolate
and I'm like those white peaches that have no color
and are just too pale!*

—Who wants to live in a world without sweet pale peaches?
says Grandma. *Besides, nothing can stop you from
being who you want to be.
You don't need to change your skin, or your height or your shape.
You just have to change the way your eyes see.*

I say nothing, but I wonder,
Who made these rules up anyway?
If someone from another planet checks in,
a thousand years from now, to study WHO our civilization
was, and WHAT we were like,
I'll leave them a letter inside the ruins that have my bones.
It'll say, *We were beautiful, so beautiful.*
*Of a beautiful color you purple-people
have never seen. Some of us were the color of fruits,
and some, the color of spices.
Some of us were as tall as young trees,
shooting, stretching as if to the sky,
and some were short and round like pearls.
Some were solid like walls*

and some quivered in the wind like feathers.
And then, magically, we could change our shapes
from skinny to fat to middling,
depending who was looking at us.
But we were all beautiful
all beautiful.
And I
was beautiful too.
That's what I'd tell those Martians
a thousand years from now.

Van Garrett and René Saldaña, Jr.
I GOT SOUL (AN I AM NOT POEM)

I am the soul that lives within.
—India

not my hair
not this skin

but
something else
something beyond   way-beyond

beyond the reach of my fingertips
beyond a tree branch's desperate grasp
beyond the clouds hanging as if by a string

all the way clear up to the stars

that's how far beyond   way-beyond
is

someplace
a place   like
my chest where all the world's stars
like a symphony of black birds
sworl

that's me
that's who I am

there   I am

23

my hair
my skin
my hands
my knuckles
my fists
my hips
my thighs
my feet
and toes

there
I am also

my gloves
my boots
the ring
the ropes
the bell to start
the bell to end

I am
the stool
the spit bucket
the spit itself
the drop of blood at my feet
the sweat soaking my shirt

there
where my soul resides
that's where I live
that's where I am
my most simple self

Luis Lopez-Maldonado
I DIDN'T ASK TO BE BROWN, I GOT LUCKY

Brown as in beautiful
as in damn, look at that hyna

Brown as in beast
as in don't mess with m' cubs

Brown as in bad
as in *no te metas con mí cucu*

Brown as in boi
as in asking to be called he/they/them

Brown as in bail
as in m' skin a free pass to jail

Brown as in ballet
as in jeté splits assemblé

Brown as in *banda*
as in closed circle *clika* gang

Brown as in blackout
as in domestic violence drugs'n'sex

Brown as in beginning
as in we were here first

Brown as in babysitter
as in growing up *Chicano*

Brown as in believability
as in seriously, I didn't do it

Brown as in bipolarization
as in *hoy no, mañana* maybe
as in I forgot to take my meds
as in it's red not burgundy
as in I'm down with d' brown
as in *café cajeta canela*
as in we are all immigrants
as in *abuelita* and *chancla* and *mija*
Because brown is brown is brown
as in the least popular Crayola color
Brown, as in aren't you brown I'm here
Brown, as in bleeding *nopal* brown
Selenas brown *Jenni* brown *Guanga* brown
Because I didn't ask to be brown
I just got lucky with my brown.

Linda Sue Park
ARBY'S, SMALL MIDWESTERN TOWN, 1967

Billboards. Screens big and little.
Book covers. Magazine pages
glossy with certainty.
Everywhere you look,
you are not there.

This is how it happens,
how your face becomes a stranger.
You see it in the mirror,
but that hardly counts

so that when you are seven years old
and walk into a restaurant with your family—
the one you go to because inside
the gleaming foil, the bread roll
softens around its filling,
reminding your parents of steamed buns—

and see another Asian family
at a table bolted to the floor,
ice rattling, foil wrappers unfurled,
your first thought is,
I wonder if they speak English?
and your second is of steamed buns.

Then your eyes widen in shock
as the truth sucks the air out of your lungs.
That's what people see when they look at us.

When they look at me.

Before that moment,
you never really knew
what you looked like.

After that moment,
you will never forget.

Jasmin Garcia
ANONYMOUS

Dear Ms. Garcia,
Today you wore shades of purple in your eyes
You carry the pride of this school on your eyelids and I love it
But sometimes I wish my brush could make the same magic
How do you get your liner to stay so sharp?
Does it take you a hundred tries before you get it right?
It takes me twelve and I'm still unsatisfied
I've tried to change the way I dress to impress my friends
I just can't keep up with the many trends from TikTok and Instagram
It's a new challenge every week but I want to look unphased just like you
How do you do it?
Today you talked to us about the book *Wonder* and the themes
You clarified that not everything is what it seems
And people of your age can be unhappy with their looks
Is it true? Do you ever feel the way I do?
You shared about what it was like for you to be fifteen
Surrounded by magazines telling you what you were expected to be
And I never noticed the faint line along your arms
That splits your skin tone into two shades, so I asked,
"Did you get bullied for looking that way?"
You said yes but the comments eventually went away
Day by day as you embraced the flaws that made you you
Because how can someone hurt you if you give them nothing to use
against you?
And I learned that I've spent so much time trying to fit the image of
Media
My parents
My friends

The other girls I envied
But never have I given permission to spend time with myself, Ms. Garcia
I think that's what you do
You take the time to listen and love yourself
Thank you.
—Anonymous

Joseph Bruchac
JIMMY STANDING BEAR

Crazy Horse
was light-skinned.
I read that in a book.
His hair was not straight,
his eyes were light,
and when he was young,
wasichus who saw him
sometimes thought that he
was a captive white kid.

His nickname,
one I think he hated,
was Curly back then
until his great vision came
and gave him a powerful name.

Grandma told me
to think about that
when other kids here
on the reservation
tease me for not
being brown enough
or call me White Bread
when my back is turned.

Crazy Horse never let anyone
take his picture or paint him,
so no one knows what he really looked like,

but I know that like me,
his blood was red
and so was his heart.

So, no matter how I look,
I know that I'll always
be part of our people.

Erika E. Garza
FEA

Sé que nunca ganaré
Un concurso de belleza
Mi madre me lo dejó claro
A mi corta edad cuando le pregunté:

-¿Soy bonita?
-No eres ni fea ni bonita.
Eres la más bonita entre las feas
O la más fea entre las bonitas.

Fue así que aprendí
que una madre puede herir al ser sincera.
En ese momento no comprendí
Su respuesta, ni su franqueza.

De niña
Todos decían que me parecía
A mi bisabuela
Por parte de mi padre…

Pero ahora que ya crecí
Cada día que pasa me parezco
Más a ella, a mi madre,
Que es el vivo retrato de mi abuela.

Yo no sé
Cuál sea su concepto de belleza
Ni si a ella también
Le dijeron lo mismo que a mí.

Pero lo que sí sé
Es que nunca daría esa respuesta
Que me dejó la autoestima por el suelo
Y me hirió en lo más profundo de mi ser...

Ahora soy mamá y mi hija es mi clon
Y siempre que puedo
Le recuerdo que es hermosa:
"You are smart and beautiful."

No importa lo que diga la gente,
Ni las revistas, ni la televisión,
Para mí, ella siempre será
la más bella versión de mí.

Sé que nunca ganaré
Un concurso de belleza,
No soy alta, ni mido 90-60-90,
No soy perfecta de pies a cabeza.

Pero sí gané muchos otros concursos
De poesía, teatro, materias...
Al fin ya comprendí que mi talento
y mi fuerza van más allá de la apariencia.

Sin querer, mi madre me hizo sentir fea
Y yo me aferré a mis otras cualidades
Y eso me hizo fuerte y valiente como ella
Y me convirtió en la mujer que ahora soy.

Erika E. Garza
FEA

I know I'll never win
A beauty contest
My mother made it clear
In my short years when I asked her,
-¿Soy bonita?
-No eres ni fea ni bonita.
Eres la más bonita entre las feas
O la más fea entre las bonitas.

"Am I pretty?"
"You are neither ugly nor pretty.
You are the prettiest among the ugly ones,
And the ugliest among the pretty ones."

It was then how I learned
That a mother can harm while being sincere.
At that moment, I did not understand
Her answer, nor her frankness.

As a girl
Everyone said I looked
Like my great grandmother
On my dad's side...

But now that I've grown up
Each day that goes by I look
More like her, my mother,
Who is the living portrait of my grandma.

I do not know
What her concept of beauty was
Or if she
Was told the same as me.

But what I do know
Is that I will never give the answer
That left my self-esteem on the floor
And hurt me deep in my soul…

I am a mom now and my daughter is my clone
And I every time I can
I remind her she is beautiful,
"Eres inteligente y hermosa."

What people say does not matter,
Neither magazines, nor television,
To me, she will always be
The most beautiful version of me.

I know I'll never win
A beauty contest,
I'm not tall, I'm not 36-24-36,
I'm not perfect from head to toe.

But I did win other contests
Of theatre, poetry, academics…
I finally understood that my talent
And my strength go beyond looks.

Unintentionally, my mom made me feel ugly
And I grappled on to my other qualities
And that made me strong and brave like her
And made me the woman I am today.

Valerie Hunter
SASQUATCH

Miri is called into Coach's office
on the fifth day of practice, his eyes
avoiding hers. "We want
a uniform look on our team,"
he says, and Miri nods, confused,
because she's wearing the uniform:
the jersey with its basketball
emblazoned like a bullseye,
the shorts that aren't exactly obscene
but are definitely a little shorter
than they need to be,
the ankle socks, the one part
of the uniform she actually likes.

"He means you need to shave,"
says Kelly, the assistant coach,
and when Miri just stares, she adds,
"Your legs. Under your arms,"
enunciating like she's talking to an idiot.

The aftermath is a blaze
of humiliation; Miri can't
remember if she nods or apologizes
or just continues staring,
but then Coach compliments
her three-point shot
and Miri backs out the door,
mumbling a thank you,

while feeling like a monster.

At home, Miri looks in the full-length mirror,
trying to see herself as others do,
prehistoric and hairy, scary, not uniform.
Has everyone been staring?
Normally she wears sleeves, leggings,
her own comfortable uniform, but now
she really looks: at the fine brown hairs
on her legs, so similar to the ones
on her arms. Who decided that leg hairs
are gross, but arm hairs are OK?
Then there are her armpits,
where the hair is patchier, coarser,
begging to be covered by sleeves.

Mom said girls in eighth grade don't need
to shave yet, a proclamation made back in August.
Mom makes many proclamations, some of which
Miri flatly disagrees with—why shouldn't
she be allowed to stay up past ten or get
her ears pierced?—but she hadn't cared about this one.
Should she tell Coach her mom won't let her?
Have Mom call Coach for a special dispensation?
She pictures the awkwardness and shudders.

The next day at practice—still hairy—
Miri spends too much time watching
the other girls, staring at their smooth legs
and underarms, until it starts to become creepy,
both her fixation and the smoothness of their skin,
plastic like Barbie dolls, everyone uniform.
She's so distracted
that she misses shots and coverage.
Coach makes her gather all the balls
afterwards, as the boys team comes out.
Miri ogles their legs, too; most—but not
all—are much hairier than hers.

As she enters the locker room, Liz Plunkett,

captain and queen of basketball,
cough-comments, "Here comes Sasquatch,"
and Miri's decision is made.
She goes home, washes her uniform,
and leaves it folded neatly
outside Coach's office the next day.
She thinks maybe someone might find her,
say something, ask her to reconsider,
but nobody does. Uniformity is everything,
and it doesn't matter how good
your three-point shot is without it.

She knows she could have made a fuss,
be the kind of girl to start a revolution,
lead a sisterhood of fuzzy-legged rebels,
but she's not that girl. She knows
she could have shaved on the sly—
Mom would never have to know—
but she's not that girl, either,
and of this she's quietly proud.

Roy Duffield

a reflection on the self reflection of a
self portrait of the poet as a young man as a self
portrait of the poet as a young man who stands before
you standing before a mirror and standing before a mirror
image of himself standing before himself standing before him
trying in vain to comb his hair into a comb parting trying in
vain to make the sides the same while his partner is trying in vain
to do the same but as hard as he tries and with all he has and
with all his might try as he might to match the sides the sides won't
match and he decides to sit out the match as a match lost is better
than a match tied as a match lost is a match won and a match
won is better than a match tied at least if you like to watch
the match which he never has done but he's done with this
parting and so takes a tie and ties it all back and back in the
mirror the mirror image takes a tie and ties it all back and
back in the back of his mind though he doesn't mind he still
has a problem the problem of his eyes which don't match as
one eye is blue and one eye is bloodshot red which
don't match his clothes and one eye is open and
the other is closed and the one eye that's open
looks at the **mirror at the mirror image** and looks
into the mirror into the one eye that's open and as
the other **that's closed** and at the door that's behind
that's **closed and that behind** which is a
hall **which ends in a hall** of mirrors without end
but every**thing comes to** an end and the poet
as a young man comes to and ends his
reflections for a second and the second
poet as a young man comes to and ends his
reflections for a second and stares at himself
and glares to himself as he doesn't even
recognise himself as the sides don't
match as one cheek is flushed with
life and one cheek is deathly pale
and one lip smiles and the other
can't and one eye sheds a tear
while the other is dry and one
eye reflects the blue day sky and
the other stares out at the stars in
the night and one side is selfish
and one side is selfless and one
bares a bare chest and the
other a stiff work shirt
collar and one has a halo
and the other a horn
and one is clean shaven
as an eight-year-old
boy and one side bares
and bears the beard of
a man of eighty years a
beard down to his knee
his knee out of shot and
you only get one shot says
the poet as a young man to
himself as a young man as he
lifts his cam' and takes his one
shot in this duel duel and it's a shot
in the dark but his hands are tied
as a duel lost is better than a duel tied
as a duel lost is a duel won and a duel won
is better than a duel tied so at least he can hold
up his head and say that he tried and look himself
squarely in the eye as a man and as a boy of eight and as an
old man of eighty and as a young man as he hates to admit but his mirror
image does look a bit like him and together they kick and they kick and they kick as both
hands wave goodbye and they both wink and there are tears in both of their eyes as they blink and a
smile on both of their pairs of lips as together they put an end to their reflections and an end to the mirror
and an end to the mirror image and an end to self portrait of the poet as a young man as a self portrait of the
poet as a young man who stands before you standing before a mirror before a door before a hall which ends in
a hall of mirrors without end and before everything within and without comes to an end and seven years of bad luck

Self-reflection

a reflection on the self reflection of a
self portrait of the poet as a young man as a self
portrait of the poet as a young man who stands before
you standing before a mirror and standing before a mirror
image of himself standing before himself standing before him
trying in vain to comb his hair into a centre parting trying in
vain to make the sides the same while his partner is trying in vain
to do the same but as hard as he tries and with all he has and
with all his might try as he might to match the sides the sides won't
match and he decides to sit out the match as a match lost is better
than a match tied as a match lost is a match won and a match
won is better than a match tied at least if you like to watch
the match which he never has done but he's done with this
parting and so takes a tie and ties it all back and back in the
mirror the mirror image takes a tie and ties it all back and
back in the back of his mind though he doesn't mind he still
has a problem the problem of his eyes which don't match as
one eye is blue and one eye is bloodshot red which
don't match his clothes and one eye is open and
the other is closed and the one eye that's open
looks at the **mirror at the mirror image** and looks
into the mirror into the one eye that's open and at
the other **that's closed** and at the door that's behind
that's **closed and that behind** which is a
hall **which ends in** a hall of mirrors without end
but every**thing comes** to an end and the poet
as a young man comes to and ends his
reflections for a second and the second
poet as a young man comes to and ends his
reflections for a second and stares at himself
and glares to himself as he doesn't even
recognise himself as the sides don't
match as one cheek is flushed with
life and one cheek is deathly pale
and one lip smiles and the other
can't and one eye sheds a tear
while the other is dry and one
eye reflects the blue day sky and
the other stares out at the stars in
the night and one side is selfish
and one side is selfless and one
bares a bare chest and the
other a stiff work shirt
collar and one has a halo
and the other a horn
and one is clean shaven
as an eight-year-old
boy and one side bares
and bears the beard of
a man of eighty years a
beard down to his knee
his knee out of shot and
you only get one shot says
the poet as a young man to
himself as a young man as he
lifts his cam' and takes his one
shot in this dual duel and it's a shot
in the dark but his hands are tied
as a duel lost is better than a duel tied
as a duel lost is a duel won and a duel won
is better than a duel tied so at least he can hold
up his head and say that he tried and look himself
squarely in the eye as a man and as a boy of eight and as an
old man of eighty and as a young man he hates to admit but his mirror
image does look a bit like him and together they kick and they kick and they kick as both
hands wave goodbye and they both wink and there are tears in both of their eyes as they blink and a
smile on both of their pairs of lips as together they put an end to their reflections and an end to the mirror
and an end to the mirror image and an end to self portrait of the poet as a young man as a self portrait of the
poet as a young man who stands before you standing before a mirror before a door before a hall which ends in
a hall of mirrors without end before everything within and without comes to an end seven years of bad luck

Sophie Stephens
IF ONLY

Baby, if you see what I see, you would never doubt again,
The mirror, your place of worship,
The sun, a lightbulb, on and off whenever you please,
Day and night they're yours,
Your lips are velvet,
Your heart, a goblet I drink from,
I carry on reading, lost in the divine script that is your skin.

Katherine Hoerth
SELF PORTRAIT AT FOURTEEN AS A DIAMONDBACK

Adolescence is a meadow and you, girl, are snake—
not sunflower, not field mouse, not baby mockingbird.

You emerged from the leathery case of childhood,
the ooze of your former self slick on your skin.

As high school approaches, you're learning
what your body can do—part the sea of grass,

coil and uncoil at will, the slender way
you move through the world inspiring fear

in the hearts of all, especially men. You taste
the venom. You feel the prick of your fangs.

The diamonds on your back sheen with beauty,
perfectly placed. You're ready to taste the world

with your forked tongue. You're ready to announce
your presence with a giggle, a rattle of your tail.

And there's a hunger deep within you, too—
to devour, to shed the skin of innocence,

reinvent yourself, new and clean, in the world
unfolding before you. There's nothing evil

in your bones, at least, not now. You'll only strike

when you hear the clang of the metal shovel,

the lawnmower's serenade, the thump of a boot,
the unwelcome touch of a stranger. Today,

you savor the venom of yourself. Today,
the world can smell your presence in the grass.

R. Joseph Rodríguez
MIRROR'S ALL IN MY BUSINESS

all up in my face
like a cyclops eye
circles around me
blinks heavy eyelids
reaches to grab me
but my body stands
up and pushes mirrors
away that just want
to talk back messy
words and say this
and that about me
words in my head
about my body
weight and mass
index from a big
fat mouth that spills
spoonfuls and ladles
of ideas into my head
muscles required
bench press this much
as if an advertisement
pop-up that nobody
can stop not even
the geeky squad
no law and order
can stop the silver
giant staring at me
somebody make

this stop once
and for all please
something there is
that finally tells me
a quiet voice there is
that does speak up
reaching out to me
to hear and listen
says to me you are
enough enough
to you and all
around you
who love you
and that is when
the mirrored voice
ceases to be inside
me like a howl
my senses wake up
and now notice
who i am and can
be and become
let it begin with me
and my head's words
and thoughts that i
can tame and keep
my body safe
and sane

—ariel, get outta there already! time to eat.

—¡ay, amá! ya voy.

Janet Wong
BABY FAT

I'm kind of chubby, but nobody really cares.
It's *baby fat*, my mother says, and laughs.

When my brother catches chickenpox,
I'm sent to live with my grandparents.
Three days later, spots pop up all over my body.
It's the most severe case the doctor has ever seen.
I am quarantined inside the apartment, not allowed out.
It's OK: every day is a parade of my favorite foods—
so perfectly fried, so crunchy, so crispy,
so savory, so sweet. I eat and eat and eat.
Next thing I know
I am thirty pounds heavier but only one inch taller.
My grandfather says I look like a rich girl now.

When my grandfather talks about his mother
and how hard she worked on the farm
and how poor they were and how hungry,
he says *skinny*
as if it were the worst thing a person could be.
She was so skinny = her life was so cursed.
I am happy to be fat like a rich girl.

But when my mother comes to get me on Labor Day,
I see shock in her eyes.
She looks at me and she is confused.
My baby, she mutters. *My baby.*
In my mind I add the word I know she is thinking,

but it is no longer funny, no longer cute.
An unspeakable word hangs in the air,
sad and alone:
fat.

Nicola Marae Allain
SKIN

Antoinette with
amber eyes
and tawny skin
sat at my side
in the blue bedroom
I shared with my brother.

We both had Tahitian
and European ancestry
but I was British white,
with blond hair and blue eyes,
and she was a beautiful
bronze brown.

I sighed and said,
"I so want to be brown like you."
"Lighter is better," she replied,
running her hand
down her arm,
before patting mine.

"There," she said,
"I gave you half my shade,
so now we'll both
be perfect."

S. Rupsha Mitra
DEAR BODY

There are days on which
barricades are placed,
shackles raised around and a convolution like some coagulation goes on there
There is no grant of soft breath, no feeling of comfort or attachment,
only gruesome images of an audience that later you might realize is imaginary—
there are days on which a raw ferocious want slithers
onto these green veins midst a bronze brownness,
a rising desire shattering the insides into pieces—a want,
to gain the shape, clarity, perfectionist priority—the
finesse of a narrow social conditioning—
this fold of tummy and saggy spiraling skin mirrors the wild side of anxiety,
the brown burnish becomes burden, yet
as in Shahid Ali's words I tell you,
Mad heart, be brave—
this brownness reminds of
the soils, the taste, the smell of my *mulk*,
this heaviness of breath, these broad thighs—breath of lionesses,
this glistering epidermis is emblazoned with courageous tales,
not bonneted, not corseted
It speaks of my emancipation.
Out of the megrim, how I soar nearer the
limitless luminosity of the expansive sky,
like a serendipity of a grand discovery, how I sigh,
to see the reflection of a home,
how I belong to you, my body, how you belong to me.

José B. González

MIDDLE SCHOOL TREMAIN

That's when I started wearing glasses
and hanging out with Johnny Tremain.
Tremain, with his burned hand that kept
him from the metals, the molten silver
that settled on his fingers, how he had
to find new work, and work without
hands, how my father had to find
new work because he had to work

with hands, how Johnny found a friend
in Rab, how Rab gave Johnny a hand,

how students in my class called me
four eyes and pushed me with their hands,

how I used the cover to Johnny Tremain
to cover my face to stop their hands,

how Johnny Tremain took my hand so
that I could learn to fight without my hands.

Zach Urquhart
INWARD

Your words, an onslaught, have hurt me in so many ways.
I tell myself your words are not about me, though,
Only about a thing about me.
Still, you hurl them,
Sharp like shards,
Words meant to
Tear through me
Or
Bore into me.
Implanting deep,
Down into my being.
I try to block them.
Still, those words can be
Pointed arrows, stinging to my very heart, making me
Feel wrong: these words, right now, all that matter to me.

Paloma Muniz-Ochoa
SPINNING

I am spinning

I am too fat
The bathing suit shows too many curves
The bathing suit looks cheap and used
I hate the color
Why did I buy this in the first place?
I should have worn makeup
My legs are too long
My arms are too short
I am too brown
I am too white
My hair is too short, I should grow it out
I have the worst color eyes

You are spinning

That is what Mom used to tell me when I was having a panic attack

Hyperventilating
Crying mountains of tears
Blood curdling screams like being fed into a woodchipper
Holding onto my table, my anchor, the only thing keeping my boat from
sinking

If I were in a sitcom

Mom would ask, "Why are you crying?"

Then after 5 seconds of talking with her I would be okay
And I would go on with that laugh track in the background and the music
to set the mood

But the thing is, life is not like that
You can't just get it over with then star in a new episode next week
And start over fresh like I had never cried
You can't just end your season on a cliffhanger
Your painful grand finale must come

This is real life
My life
My feelings are a fan in my mind
I picture myself tapping the blades with my hand even though it hurts
I keep tapping and tapping and tapping until it eventually stops
spinning
How do I wake up
How do I take the blindfold off to see my real life?

We are all spinning

I take a deep breath
The fan eventually stops
Today, this is *my* beach
this is *my* body
these are *my* curves
this is *my* face
these are *my* long legs
these are *my* short arms
this is the color of *my* skin
this is *my* hair
these are *my* eyes

I have to feel my feelings
to be able to let them go
And that is how

I stop spinning

Dorothy Neagle
THE HISTORY OF THE SIREN

after Gustav Wertheimer's 'The Kiss of the Siren'

My mother's loom stood open
upstairs in the old house
where I was not allowed to go
with ribs of yarn, some close
and some set far apart.
I longed to see the end
of what she wove, but
we moved out, packed up
all the scraps of fabric
and the loom became a ghost.

I'd been told of the women
who lived in the ocean
resting on rocks at the furthest
edges of the sea, their skin
a seafoam spectrum. I didn't
ask my mother about them.
I sensed it was a thing
all women knew, like
no matter how much a man's
story about them changed,
it wasn't true. Some men
told that the women were lonely
because they were dangerous.
I was only jealous that when
a storm came up, they slipped
below the water and took

danger for their refuge.

It was known they lived on song
and when they opened their mouths,
water poured out. For centuries
men searched for ways to
kill them. When sailors saw
a siren rise and ride along
the boat side, plastered like
a starfish, her peach skin flayed
and pulsing, looking almost
dead but also like the only living
thing, the sailors' mouths would
open and they'd lean out.
I think they envied
what their own dry throats
would never know: how it feels
to breathe right through the drowning.

By the time I was alive
the women had been written
into mermaids by men who
failed to tame them. But many
land women are also whales
and we know the language
they made up between them, the
calls that pierce the silence and the flesh,
the songs that are the key to
staying alive beneath the water.
By myself at day or night, I'd
climb away to lift my face up to
the sky and wait for her to open
her lips, for the water to fall down
into my mouth, the fountain of
sound reminding me
no matter how much I ate,
I would always be hungry.

Genoa Yáñez-Alaniz

DAUGHTER OF PURITY

I was taught early on to hide the shape
the shame in the blood
to wear skin taut
over bones half starved

An eight-mile run
under 600 calories
kept the curves from the cling
skin hidden in the shade
soaked in milk
bleached with lemon
a temporary whitewash

I   from filtered ritual
cotton field blues sung
in faded antebellum dress
the shed of esclavitud
unchained skin
through marriage
to Mestizos and Kikapú

Caramel skin was born from fear
pelo liso escaped the roots
an ancestral assimilation
of las Negras Puras
Las Mascogas de Nacimiento México
Nacimiento de los negros

And I have come full circle

my daughter born true
no hiding the history of her curves
the fullness of lips
skin beautiful and bronze

The sun touches down on her dance
afro rhythm finds a home at her hips
her body fluid beauty of muscle and strength
adorned with gold and silver
unlocked cuffs from her wrists

She wears the celebration of our ancestors
The grit
The reach for survival
The power
The vibrancy
…her crown

Nikki Grimes
ACTIONS SPEAK

Some say they dislike your complexion,
but watch the girl on the beach,
slathering her pale epidermis
with expensive suntan lotion,
apparently subscribing to the notion
that your melanin rich skin
is to be desired, if only for a season.

Need another reason
to refuse to buy their lies?
Some disparage each African feature,
declaring you an ugly creature,
yet, investing serious coin to get
lip, hip, and butt injections—
a vain attempt to replicate
the fabulous fullness and curves
nature already blessed you with.

Others denigrate your crown on the daily—
your nappy hair, braids and dreads.
Note: their poisonous barbs
are all of a similar thread,
meant to detract from your beauty.
But then they race to the hair salon
to transform their manes
into some semblance of your braids,
afro, or desperate version of dreads,
as if their overworked locks

could ever look like yours.

Forget whatever ugliness some spew
to deny your Black beauty.
What is it they say about imitation?
It's the sincerest form
of flattery.

Crystal Stewart
FINDING MY WINGS

That first day of high school
I must have looked a sight
My face one big freckle,
my fringe cut too high
A pimple pulsing on my chin,
a seething volcano set to erupt.

At recess I ran for the restroom
Three girls crowded the mirror
posing for selfies
Lip gloss and kohl-rimmed eyes
Their cheekbones contoured
to within an inch of their lives
All I felt was envy.

I could barely hold my head up
and smile at a boy without
blushing and sweating
The dimples on my face
reduced me to a baby
I felt plain and awkward,
bony and ungainly.

My mom would say:
Girl, you're at the pupa stage
like a caterpillar picking
its own unique palette
Then would someone please

pass me my cocoon
till I'm hatched out and ready?

Back at the Girls room
the last cubicle was free
I perched there to weep
I didn't want unique
I wanted the swagger and grace
of the girls in their clique
Their hitched-up hems
and caramel thighs
Their pearl white nails
tapping emojis
to the wanting boys.

From the next stall, a girl stepped out
pushing a hanky up her sleeve
She stood at the sink,
dragged a brush through her hair
and flashed me a gunmetal grin
She asked me my name,
whose class I was in?

We sat together at lunch
and laughed at the boys
locked in their wrestling bouts
like they'd never left kindergarten
Some things never change.

And the moment
I stepped outside myself
I met with the answer
We're all too busy hatching
to see each other's fluttering
Even the pretty girls
have to learn the word NO
when the boys ask for more
than they're ready to give.

The dimples soon fade,

we outgrow the training bra,
remove the brace
We find a shade of make-up
that hides what we can't face
This becoming is just the beginning
The caterpillar can't fly,
yet there's flight in her DNA

She is finding her wings.

Julia Perez
BECAUSE I'M A WOMAN

Edward Vidaurre
ODE TO THE GIRL WHO TOLD ME SHE WOULD DATE ME IF I LOST WEIGHT

she was always talking
she knew everyone and
we had a class together in
high school, she wore braces
that caused her to suck
on her teeth between words
in high school I was more of a
people watcher, a bit shy
her name rhymes with flower
and was bussed to school
from South Central L.A.
her long hair hung down her back
almost reaching the ground
when she sat on the plastic chair
in Algebra class. She smelled of
powder and strawberry lip gloss
she always knew the answers and
I cheated from her from time to time and
only when I cared to finish the work
she thought me as cute
I once told her her hair was pretty
asked if it took long to brush
she said, what do you think?
I crawled into myself and carved
our names inside my intestines
until I excused myself to throw up
her friends were popular too

cheerleaders, drama, yearbook,
music, and everything else that makes
them stay after school
that year I started skipping school a lot
I was drifting and making no sense of myself
wandering the streets bored
wishing the truant police would catch me and
set me straight, they never came
and I walked the streets spilling my youth
I spoke with homeless men and they would always say,
"go back to school, give me money," or just sat in
silence with me in a daze on pissed pants and torn shoes
the girl whose name rhymes with flower
said she would date me if I lost weight
but I said, "I wouldn't date you right now that I'm fat,
you remind me of the time I sucked my teeth
at my dad and he left belt welts on my back."

Genoa Wilson

ANA

You are
so busy
not eating.
Holding
the light
in your hands
to twist
into twilight,
to taste
a spangle
of night.
Morning comes
with a yawn
in your gullet
and only air
to carry you
through the day.

Abril Garcia-Linn
THESE THINGS

These things, poking out of my blouse. They have a mind of their own. Calling men, women and children to look at them. Sometimes to stare and every now and then, to make comments or even to touch them.

Once, on a crowded bus on the way home from high school, a man came up to me before his stop. He tapped my shoulder and loudly professed his feelings for them. What could I do but cower under the weight of them? They seemed to speak for me. To call out to people. I was too embarrassed to look around and see the expressions on the other passengers' faces. Were they angry? Did they laugh? I wanted to evaporate from the heat of shame.

That boy in 5th grade that I thought was my friend, was mesmerized by them. I would often turn my chair around to talk to him. He was kind and funny. Until that fateful day when he suddenly poked them. He said he wanted to see what they felt like. I pretended it didn't happen. What gave him permission? Was my blouse too shear? All I know is, I didn't want it.

Then the touches began to come from my Padrino. Always buying me gifts, treating me special. When we were alone, his hands did not rest. I said nothing, and no one else seemed to notice or care. I froze. Every time. Dreaded every encounter. Told myself he was overly affectionate.

As I became an adult, they grew larger, so large they even offended people. At times I received unwanted "advice" from women to surgically alter my body. "Why don't you get a breast reduction?" The first time a woman suggested this I was horrified. It came from an older woman, my boss. She could not look at me without a perverse filter in her mind. "At least wear a scarf," she said.

As I matured, I began to embrace my curves, enjoy the way my clothes draped my body. I stopped allowing comments and cruel gazes to hurt me. I took control of my body, refused the touches of those who had no permission, and enjoyed the sensual touches of those that I desired. I eventually came to love what I used to think were foreign objects with a mind of their own. Finally, my breasts were part of me. Finally, they were mine.

Daniel García Ordaz
CORPORAL CADENCE

(for U.S. Army Spc. Vanessa Guillén)

Atten- . . . tion!

Parade . . . rest!
  Parade best.
  Parade test.
  Parade chest.

A ten- . . . sion!

About . . . face!
  Small waist.
  Make haste.
  Can't waste.

Left . . . face!
  Debase.
  Disgrace.
  Open case.

Right . . . face!
  Pretty face.
  Made-up face.
  Soft as lace.

Mark time . . . march!
  Nighttime arch.
  Full lips parch.
  Wrinkled starch.

Ready . . . halt!
  Pour salt.
  It's your fault.
  Cement vault.

About . . . face!
  About race.
  About chase.
  About base.

Forward . . . march!

Ariane Ambriz

MI MADRE

Mi madre
Like a leather whip across your face
demands the utmost respect
Or else

Red lips, pencil skirt
Hear the sound of her stilettos
Piercing every heart
Of her opposers

Which sometimes now is me

I often yielded to her
More than needed
And thought two, three steps ahead
To avoid the wrath
Of the stressed single mother

Anxieties & depressions
are for the weak
Don't stress me out
No ves que estoy ocupada
She would speak

I want a drink
Glass, spotless
Ice, cubed & clear
Bottle, never from a can
Loudly spoken demands

Dress too tight
Dress too loose
Flats instead of heels?
Derecha la flecha
Earrings don't match
That necklace is too much
Anti-wrinkle cream ASAP
Size 2,4,6
Maybe 8
14? Please God! No!
Here's a size 4
Make it your goal
I believe if you believe
Why didn't you wear the other dress?

My poems have never betrayed.

But now, it's too late.

Linda McCauley Freeman
BODY, SHAME, BEAUTY, THEFT

School is over for the summer.
It is the worst time of year.

I am fifteen and believe my body
indistinguishable from a pencil.

My best friend, Lisa, shows off
her new yellow bikini and blossomed body.

I lie on her bed

thinking of all the suits I tried
strewn in dressing room stalls,

the $65 padded purple one-piece
I finally stuffed deep inside my purse.

When we go to the beach I hide under towels.
She has grown so beautiful men stare at her.

I walk slightly behind
so I don't disappoint their view.

The next year we will no longer be friends
because of this.

She tries to make me feel better by calling
herself ugly. The year we are no longer friends

she will get a nose job.

Katharyn Salsman
S K I N

The compliment is veiled,
I wish I could eat whatever I wanted
If I looked like you, I would never have to work out
I could never wear something like that
But each compliment is
Shrouded in jealousy
Dripping with judgement
And means the same thing
You are   s k i n n y.

To be *s k i n n y* is a weight to carry
To be *s k i n n y* is to be the model image for young girls
To be *s k i n n y* is to continue to fit in the mold because
If I wasn't *s k i n n y*, what would people compliment me on?
Surely not my intelligence
Nor my achievements
Never mind my talents
It always seems to be centered around the weight
Which is not really a compliment at all.

Padma Venkatraman
AMERICAN BEAUTY

When I first heard a boy exclaim, with reverence, "She's an all-American beauty,"
I thought all it meant was she'd never had to enter an immigration office.
When he explained (unquestioning, unhesitating) "blonde and blue-eyed" I felt
ashamed   and sorry   for *him* for missing   ALL   American beauty.

Melina Melgoza

DAMAGED

Jenn Givhan

BODY IMAGE, OR NIEVE REMINDS ME WHO I AM

If the earth were flat
        you could spot a candle flickering
        from thirty miles away.

When you blush
        the lining of your stomach
        blushes too.

You contain more atoms
        than stars in our galaxy.

Thousands of years ago
        you ran after prey
        until it died of exhaustion.

You could run for that long.

Each hour
        you release enough heat
        to boil water.

A block of your bone
        just a matchbox of your bone
        could support
        nine elephants.

You are bioluminescent.
You glow in the dark—

If you could pick up the light
         with your illusionist's eyes
         you would see
         who you are—

You would see who you are
         & marvel.

CONTRIBUTORS:

Raised in Papeete, Tahiti, French Polynesia, **NICOLA MARAE ALLAIN** grew up to the rhythms of ancestral drums, senses heightened by the perfume of gardenias and the scent of the sea. Nicola shares stories from her British-Polynesian ancestry and rich family history in narrative memoir poems. She is the Dean of the School of Arts and Humanities at SUNY Empire State College.

ARIANE AMBRIZ was born and raised in Houston, TX. She earned her BA in English from UT-Austin and her M.A. in Spanish Translation & Interpreting from UT-RGV. She wrote her first poem at age 6 and was first published at age 37. She has never given up on her dream to continue writing and publishing. Ariane lives in Cypress, TX, with her husband and two sons. After teaching and surviving cancer twice, she is now working on her debut novel.

DESPY BOUTRIS's writing has been published or is forthcoming in *American Poetry Review, American Literary Review, The Journal, Copper Nickel, Colorado Review, Prairie Schooner*, and elsewhere. Currently, she teaches at the University of Houston, works as Assistant Poetry Editor for *Coast*, and serves as Editor-in-Chief of *The West Review*.

An enrolled member of the Nulhegan Abenaki Nation, **JOSEPH BRUCHAC** is a writer and traditional storyteller. Author of over 170 books in several genres, his numerous awards include the Lifetime Achievement Award from The Native Writers Circle of the Americas.

JOSEPHINE CÁSAREZ is a native of San Antonio, TX. In 1979, she was a founding member of the Latina literary group Mujeres Grandes that published two anthologies of poetry and prose. Her talent as a writer and poet allowed her to perform at several universities throughout the United States. Josephine moved to California in 1996 to study comedy in Los Angeles under Barry Neal. In 1998 she returned to San Antonio and starred in the first historic

Latina comedy show at the Guadalupe Theatre. Josephine has worked in special education support for the San Antonio Independent School District.

A retired educator, ENEDINA C. VÁSQUEZ is an author, poet, and playwright as well as a world-renowned artist. Cásarez Vásquez has exhibited her art in the United States, Mexico, Europe, and Japan. She has shown her art in the *Chicano Now* exhibit at the Smithsonian. Her first book, a collection of personal vignettes and accompanying artwork, was published in 1980, and is titled *Recuerdos de una niña*.

ROY DUFFIELD was honored to perform at Barcelona Beat Poetry Festival 2019 alongside some of Spain's most successful contemporary performance poets. His work has recently appeared (or soon will) in *The Trouvaille Review*, *Night Bus to Speakers' Corner*, *PoENtry Slam*, *Flashes of Brilliance*, *Anti-Heroin Chic*, *Pure Slush*, *Half-baked*, *The Dawntreader* and an as yet untitled anthology to raise money for Marie Curie nurses during the coronavirus pandemic. He sometimes posts some micropoetry as @drinking_traveller.

MARGARITA ENGLE is the Cuban-American author of verse books such as *The Surrender Tree*, *Enchanted Air*, *Forest World*, and *Drum Dream Girl*. Awards include the NSK Neustadt Prize, three Astrid Lindgren Award Nominations, a Newbery Honor, multiple Pura Belpré, Walter, Américas, Jane Addams, and International Latino Book Awards and Honors, as well as the Charlotte Zolotow, PEN USA, Golden Kite, Green Earth, Lee Bennett Hopkins, Arnold Adoff, and Claudia Lewis Awards, among others. Margarita served as the 2017-2019 Young People's Poet Laureate. Her most recent books include *With a Star in My Hand*, *Dreams From Many Rivers*, and *Dancing Hands*. Forthcoming books include *Your Heart, My Sky*, and *A Song of Frutas*. Margarita was born in Los Angeles, but developed a deep attachment to her mother's homeland during childhood summers with relatives on the island. She studied agronomy and botany along with creative writing, and now lives in central California with her husband.

www.margaritaengle.com
Facebook: Margarita Engle
Twitter: @margaritapoet
Instagram: @engle.margarita

GIANA GALLARDO HESTERBERG is the author of a 40-day devotional, *Stories by the Seashore*, and a children's book, *Music, Music, You Can Too!* She is currently a piano teacher in the Rio Grande Valley of South Texas. Her writing has appeared in *Woman's World*, *The Mighty*, *Earnest*, and *God-sized Dreams*. You can find her occasionally contributing to her blog, *storiesbytheseashore.com*.|

JASMIN GARCIA is a Rio Grande Valley-based poet. Her works can be found published in *La Bloga* (2017) and *VIPF Boundless Anthology* (2018). Garcia has read at venues across the RGV and hopes to publish her own book someday. For the meanwhile, her works can be found on her Instagram, @thecafepoet.

ABRIL GARCIA-LINN is a proud Chicana from San Antonio, TX. She is an artist, writer, performer, and teacher. She is a founding member of the poetry/performance group Women of Ill Repute:Refute. Her poems are published in several anthologies including *Cantos Al Sexto Sol: An Anthology of Aztlanahuac Writing* and the forthcoming *Poetry for Contemporary Chicanx Writers Anthology*. Her original play *The Altar* was showcased at the San Antonio Museum of Art in 2019.

TEDx Speaker **DANIEL GARCÍA ORDAZ**, a.k.a. The Poet Mariachi, a Texas-based teacher and author from McAllen, is an established voice in Latino and Mexican American poetry. His work has been taught and written about by academics across the U.S. and abroad, and he is a 2018 Pushcart Prize nominee. García has an MFA in Creative Writing from The University of Texas Rio Grande Valley. He is also a singer/songwriter, former journalist, photographicationisticator, and word-maker-upper. García appears in the documentary, *ALTAR: Cruzando fronteras/Building bridges*. He is the founder of the Rio Grande Valley Int'l. Poetry Festival. García served in the U.S. Navy as a Hospital Corpsman. His individual book titles include the #1 bestseller books and ebook *You Know What I'm Sayin'?* and *Centzontle/Mockingbird: Songs of Empowerment* (and its YA version), as well as the #1 bestseller ebook *Pet Names*. He's presently at work on a children's poetry manuscript. García's work has appeared in several journals and anthologies.

VAN GARRETT teaches African American Studies and Literature at University of Houston. A graduate of the New York's Fashion Institute of Technology's Sneaker Essentials program, Van is an award-winning author whose work is appreciated around the world. He is the author of several collections of poetry, including *Songs in Blue Negritude*, *LENNOX IN TWELVE*, *HOG*,

ZURI: Love Songs, Pit Bulls and J-Walks, and *Water Bodies*. Additionally, he has co-authored with Ran Walker the multi-genre book, *Can I Kick It?* mixing Garrett's poetry with Walker's micro-prose. His debut picture book, *Kicks* (Versity/HMH), is slated for fall 2022 publication. He can be reached at www.vangarrettpoet.com.

ERIKA ELISA GARZA is originally from the magic town Cd. Mier, Tamaulipas, México. She holds a Master's Degree of Arts in Spanish from UTPA with a thesis focusing in creative writing of short stories. Garza is currently a Spanish Dual Instructor at La Joya ISD and South Texas College. Her poems have been published in the *FEIPOL* Anthology 2018 Edition, *Boundless 2019*, *Boundless 2020*, *Dreaming: A Tribute to Selena Quintanilla-Pérez*, and *FAME RGV Magazine*.

JENN GIVHAN, a Mexican-American poet who has received NEA and PEN/ Rosenthal Emerging Voices fellowships, is the author of two novels and four full-length collections of poetry, most recently *Rosa's Einstein* (University of Arizona Press) and *Trinity Sight* (Blackstone Publishing), and her work has appeared in *The Nation*, *The New Republic*, *Poetry*, *Salon*, and many others.

RODNEY GOMEZ was born and raised in Brownsville, TX. He earned a BA from Yale University, an MA in philosophy from Arizona State University, an MFA from the University of Texas Pan American, and an MPA from the University of Texas Rio Grande Valley. His collections include *Arsenal with Praise Song* (Orison Books, 2020), *Geographic Tongue* (Pleiades Press, 2020), winner of the Pleiades Press Visual Poetry Series, *Ceremony of Sand* (YesYes Books, 2019), and *Citizens of the Mausoleum* (Sundress Publications, 2018). He is the winner of the Drinking Gourd Chapbook Poetry Prize, the Gloria E. Anzaldúa Poetry Prize, and the Rane Arroyo Chapbook Prize. Gomez is a member of the Macondo Writers' Workshop and edits an annual anthology for youth poets from the lower Rio Grande Valley. He works in mobility demand management as Executive Director of Parking and Transportation at the University of Texas Rio Grande Valley and lives in McAllen, TX, where he serves as poet laureate.

JOSÉ B. GONZÁLEZ is the author of *Toys Made of Rock* and *When Love Was Reels*. His poetry has been published in the *Norton Introduction to Literature* and *The Wandering Song: Central American Writing in the United States* and in journals including *Callaloo*, *Palabra*, and *Acentos Review*. A Fulbright

Scholar, he is the co-editor of *Latino Boom: An Anthology of U.S. Latino Literature* and editor of LatinoStories.Com.

New York Times bestselling author **NIKKI GRIMES** is the recipient of the 2020 ALAN Award for significant contributions to young adult literature, the 2017 Children's Literature Legacy Award for substantial and lasting contributions to literature for children, the 2016 Virginia Hamilton Literary Award, and the 2006 NCTE Award for Excellence in Poetry for Children. The author of Coretta Scott King Author Award-winner *Bronx Masquerade*, and recipient of five CSK Author Honors, her most recent titles include the much-honored *Words With Wings*, *Garvey's Choice* and Boston Globe-Horn Book honor, *Between the Lines*, and *One Last Word*, winner of the 2018 Lee Bennett Hopkins Poetry Award. Her 2019 memoir *Ordinary Hazards*, won both a Printz Honor and a Sibert Honor. Her most recent book is the best-selling and timely picture book *Kamala Harris: Rooted in Justice* (illustrated by Laura Freeman).

KATHERINE HOERTH is the author of four poetry collections, including *Goddess Wears Cowboy Boots*, which won the Helen C. Smith Prize for the best book of poetry in Texas in 2015. She is an Assistant Professor of English at Lamar University and serves as Editor-in-Chief of Lamar University Literary Press. In fall 2020, her next poetry collection, *Borderland Mujeres*, will be released by SFAU Press. The book is a bilingual collection of feminist poetry and art collaboratively created with poet Julieta Corpus and artist Corinne McCormack Whittemore.

VALERIE HUNTER teaches high school English and has an MFA in writing for children and young adults from Vermont College of Fine Arts. Her stories and poems have appeared in publications including *Cricket*, *Cicada*, *Other Voices*, *(Re)Sisters*, and *Brave New Girls*. "Sasquatch" was inspired by a letter she saw in an advice column and her own frequent antipathy towards shaving.

LUIS LOPEZ-MALDONADO is a Xicanx poeta, choreographer, and educator, born and raised in Southern California. He earned a Bachelor of Arts degree from the University of California Riverside, in Creative Writing and Dance. His poetry has been seen in *The American Poetry Review*, *Foglifter*, *The Packinghouse Review*, *Public Pool*, and *Latina Outsiders: Remaking Latina Identity*, among many others. He also earned a Master of Arts degree in Dance from Florida State University and a Master of Fine Arts degree in Creative

Writing from the University of Notre Dame, where he was poetry editorial assistant for the *Notre Dame Review*, and founder of the men's writing workshop in the St. Joseph County Juvenile Justice Center, he is the recipient of the Sparks Summer Fellowship 2016. He is currently adding his glitter to the Land of Enchantment, working for the public education system, and preparing for acceptance to The University of New Mexico, School of Law, where he plans to pursue immigration, criminal, and personal injury law.

LINDA MCCAULEY FREEMAN has been widely published in international literary journals and anthologies, including a Chinese translation of her work. Most recently she appeared in *Poet Magazine, Amsterdam Quarterly*, won Grand Prize in StoriArts poetry contest honoring Maya Angelou, and was selected by the Arts MidHudson for their Poets Respond to Art 2020 show. She was a three-time winner in the Talespinners Short Story contest judged by Michael Korda. She has an MFA in Writing and Literature from Bennington College and is the former poet-in-residence of the Putnam Arts Council. She lives in the Hudson Valley, NY. She is working on a young adult novel. You can follow her at www.Facebook.com/LindaMcCauleyFreeman.

MELINA MELGOZA is a public school teacher, activist, and writer in Los Angeles, CA. Though born and raised in Los Angeles, her roots come from a small town called Ayotlán, Jalisco, Méx. The long history of the *pueblo*'s conquest is evident in its Nahuatl name. As a teacher in the second largest district in the United States, she works to develop students' critical consciousness, critical hope, and resilience through Ethnic Studies. As an activist, she fights for a more just world. As a writer, she brings her words to life through her stories and poems. Her first book of poetry is *Border Scars* (2020).

S. RUPSHA MITRA is a student of Psychology Honours from India. She loves writing poetry and has a penchant for everything that is creative. She successfully completed her first Poetry Marathon this year. Her works have appeared in *Blue Marble Review, Indian Periodical, Harbinger Asylum*, and *Hebe Poetry Magazine*.

PALOMA MUÑIZ-OCHOA is 11 years old and lives in Pasadena, CA. She enjoys writing and singing spontaneously. She has three moms, two dogs, and one cat. She is passionate about social justice, supporting small businesses, and vanilla ice cream. Her favorite thing to do is spend time with her friends and family.

Dorothy Neagle is a Kentuckian who lives and writes in New York. She has studied writing most recently at the Unterberg Poetry Center, and her poetry has appeared or is forthcoming in *Tiny Spoon, The Fieldstone Review, Tilde, Semicolon,* and more. Her nonfiction has appeared in *Memoirist, The Nasiona,* and the *Dead Mule School of Southern Literature.* You can find her on Instagram: @sentencesaremyfave.

Mason Nunemaker is a graduate of the University of Minnesota where he earned a BA in English, an emphasis in poetry writing. As an undergraduate student, he was an officer of the U of M's slam poetry organization and represented them twice at the College Unions Poetry Slam Invitational (CUPSI). His work has been featured in *Goliath Magazine, The Miscreant, the minnesota review,* and on the *Indiefeed Performance Poetry* Podcast. He lives in Minneapolis.

Linda Sue Park is the author of many books for young readers, including the 2002 Newbery Medal winner *A Single Shard* and the NYTimes bestseller *A Long Walk to Water.* Her most recent titles include *Prairie Lotus,* a historical fiction middle-grade novel, and *The One Thing You'd Save,* a collection of linked poems. The daughter of Korean immigrants, Linda Sue created the KiBooka list--Kids' Books by Korean Americans (and Korean diaspora)-- and hosts the KiBooka page on her website. She grew up in Illinois, and has traveled widely to promote books and reading. Linda Sue knows very well that she will never be able to read every great book ever written, but she keeps trying anyway. Visit her website at www.lindasuepark.com; follow her on Twitter @LindaSuePark.

Julia Perez is a high school senior in the Dallas, TX area. Her love of photography, poetry, and social justice brought her to this visual poem. After graduation, she plans to pursue a degree, though she is still undecided as to a major. Her work can be seen on Instagram: @Jules.photos.14.

R. Joseph Rodríguez was born and raised in Houston, TX. He is the author of poetry, fiction, and nonfiction. His most recent book project is titled *This Is Our Summons Now,* a poetry collection. Joseph is coeditor of *English Journal.* He lives and teaches in Austin, TX. Follow him @escribescribe.

René Saldaña, Jr. is the author of several books for young adults, including *The Jumping Tree, A Good Long Way,* and *Heartbeat of the Soul of* *the World*. His poems have appeared in *English Journal, Windward Review, The Poetry Friday Anthology of Celebrations*, and *Living Beyond Borders*. He is associate professor in Curriculum and Instruction at Texas Tech University. With Van Garrett, he is co-authoring a novel-in-verse about two young female boxers. Saldaña is also the editor of this anthology.

KATHARYN SALSMAN grew up in Denton, TX and currently lives in Lubbock, TX. She is working on her master's degree in education and teaches fourth grade reading/writing. She has a nonfiction piece in Texas Tech University's *The Harbinger*, a Tiny Truth in *Creative Nonfiction issue 70*, and a poem in the online literary journal *TEJASCOVIDO*. Salsman enjoys rollerblading around the block and spending time with her dog, Bubbles.

SOPHIE STEPHENS has been writing ever since she knew how to. At the age of six she was already producing "novels" such as *When the World Turned to Chocolate* and writing and producing plays for the family on a Saturday night with the authority of a big time director. Writing has always been an integral part of her life, and without it she doesn't feel like she is truly herself. With her writing, her only hope really is to help others, in similar ways to how it helps her. Writing as a form of healing. She features much of her writing on Instagram under @fringepoetry, which is a day by day snippet into her experiences.

CRYSTAL STEWART lives in the North of England and is a playwright and creative producer. Her plays *Garden of the Heart* and *Peacock Boy* toured with Boojum theatre. The pandemic has led her back to her first loves, poetry and prose. Recent writing credits include *Indigo, In Parentheses* (July 2020) and *Evergreen, Pure Slush* (published Oct 2020).

CARMEN TAFOLLA is the author of more than thirty books, recipient of many international and national awards, State Poet Laureate of Texas 2015, and a Professor Emeritus of Bicultural-Bilingual Studies at the University of Texas San Antonio.

ZACH URQUHART, an educator who has previously published articles in *NOW Magazine* and *Focus Daily News*, is a Curriculum Specialist and Instructional Coach in Midlothian, TX. He is currently a doctoral student in the Language, Diversity & Literacy Studies program at Texas Tech University, where he is focusing on examining how diverse literature can inform privilege and Whiteness. He can be found on Twitter @zurquhart.

Padma Venkatraman was an oceanographer, diversity director, teacher and head of school before becoming a full-time writer. She is the author of four award-winning novels: *The Bridge Home, Climbing the Stairs, Island's End,* and *A Time To Dance* (which is a verse novel), and several poems (including, most recently, a tanka contribution to the *ThankU: Poems of Gratitude* anthology). Visit her at www.padmavenkatraman.com, @padmatv (Twitter) and venkatraman.padma (Ig, Fb).

Edward Vidaurre is the author of seven collections of poetry. He is the 2018-2019 City of McAllen, TX Poet Laureate, a five-time Pushcart-nominated poet, and publisher of FlowerSong Press. His writings have appeared in *The New York Times, The Texas Observer, Grist, Poet Lore, The Acentos Review, Poetrybay, Voices de la Luna,* as well as other journals and anthologies. Vidaurre is from Boyle Heights, CA, and now resides in McAllen, TX, with his wife and daughter.

Genoa Wilson struggled throughout her teens with anorexia and is especially pleased to be part of this project. She is a member of the Downtown Writers Center in Syracuse, NY. Her poetry has appeared in *Ghost City Review* and *Stone Canoe,* and is forthcoming in *Right Hand Pointing One Sentence Poems.*

Janet Wong is the author of more than 30 books for children and teens on a wide variety of subjects, including identity (*A Suitcase of Seaweed & MORE*) and yoga (*Twist: Yoga Poems*). With co-author Sylvia Vardell, she has created several interactive anthologies that are also writing journals, such as *HERE WE GO: A Poetry Friday Power Book.* Learn more about her at JanetWong.com.

Genoa Yáñez-Alaniz promotes refugee and immigrant social integration through community activism. She is the Co-Founder of Welcome: A Poetry Declaration: a platform for refugee and immigrant voices in partnership with San Antonio (TX) Immigration Liaison's Office. New to submitting her poetry, she has been published in *The Journal of Latina Critical Feminism, Cutthroat: A Journal of the Arts Anthology of Contemporary Chicanx Writing,* and named a finalist for the Kallisto Gaia Press Julia Darling Memorial Poetry Prize. She has an upcoming publication for the 2020 Annual Kathmandu Conference on Nepal and the Himalaya Proceedings entitled

Immigrant Communities, Sustainable Living and CIELO Gardens: Bhutanese Refugees in San Antonio.